Waterfowl Postcard Colle

Kit Howard Breen

Voyageur Press

Published by Voyageur Press, Inc.
123 North Second Street
Stillwater, MN 55082 USA

ISBN 0-89658-144-6

Printed in Hong Kong

For a free catalog of books write or call:
Voyageur Press
123 North Second Street
Stillwater, MN 55082 USA
1-800-888-9653
In MN: 612-430-2210

89 90 91 92 93 5 4 3 2 1

There was a time when postcards were bought by travelers and sent to those at home with a "wish you were here!" Often the postcards were boring and seldom were they kept. Fortunately, times have changed, and so have postcards. Now we collect as well as send postcards. It's no wonder, with cards such as these!

Here, the beauty and elegance of North America's waterfowl has been captured in a collection of waterfowl postcards by noted nature photographer Kit Howard Breen. The artist's dedication to the conservation of these magnificent birds and their natural habitats can be seen in these breathtaking portraits. Here are cheerful, clowning Snow Geese; a blast of autumn colors and their feathered admirers; a Green Wing Teal; a Canada Goose with goslings; a Hooded Merganser; a Great Blue Heron with a Sunfish — and more. Send these to nature and photography lovers or keep for your own wildlife art collection!

Kit Howard Breen's wonderful sense of waterfowl photography comes from her dedication to artistic yet scientifically accurate portrayals of her subjects. She spent some time early in life learning drawing and watercolor painting, developing a sense of form and composition. Initially, she photographed landscapes and marine scenes. In 1980, she began photographing ducks and geese on the eastern shore of Maryland, finding wildlife photography a more interesting challenge. Breen has a strong commitment to conservation, belonging to a number of conservation organizations. Although she is not a hunter, she is a contributor to Ducks Unlimited because they have done so much to preserve wetlands for waterfowl.

Breen lives in Annandale, Virginia, and her work takes her all over North America. She has conducted workshops and slide presentations for the National Wildlife Federation and the National Zoo in Washington, D.C., and has earned numerous awards, including four first place awards for "Twilight Landing." She has exhibited photographs at both the Southeastern and the Northeastern Wildlife Expositions, the 50th North American Wildlife and Natural Resources Conference, and has had one artist shows for The National Wildlife Federation and Colorfax Galleries. Her photos have appeared in the *Audubon Calendar, Reader's Digest, Ducks Unlimited, Country Magazine, Fairfax Magazine,* and *Birder's World,* among others. Breen has been co-editor of the popular *Waterfowl Calendar* since 1983, and is the author of *Photographing Waterfowl: Techniques for the Advanced Amateur and Professional.*

Canada Goose with Grasses

Canvasback Splash

Green Wing Teal

Canada Goose with Goslings

Great Blue Heron with Sunfish

Black Bellied Tree Duck

Canada Geese Flying

Windy Woody

Mute Swans

Snow Goose Family

Western Grebes Courtship Dance

Hooded Merganser

Fulvous Tree Duck

From *The Waterfowl Postcard Collection.* Copyright © 1989 By
E. & P. Bauer. Voyageur Press, 123 N. 2nd St., Stillwater MN 55082

Mallards' Ballet Company

Great Blue Heron

Blue Wing Teal

Snow Goose Clowns

Ruddy Duck

Mallard Flying In

American Wigeon

Tundra Swans Flight

Twilight Landing

Mallard in Snow Storm

Swimming Woodduck

Mallard Duckling

Gadwall

Black Duck in Snow

Canada Gosling

Pintail in Marsh